AF470630

PRE-RAPHAELITES

AND THEIR FOLLOWERS

PRE-RAPHAELITES

AND THEIR FOLLOWERS

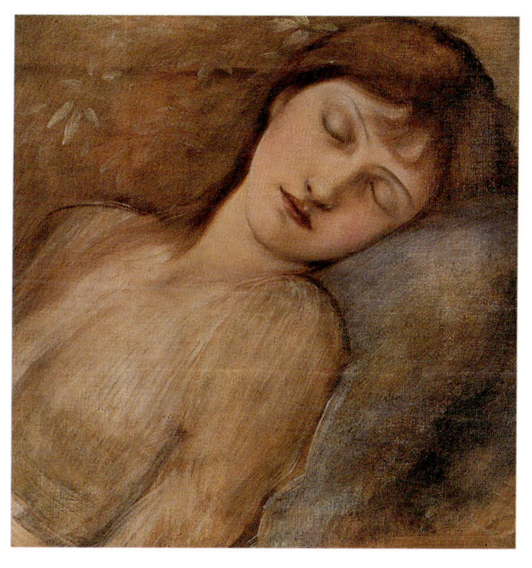

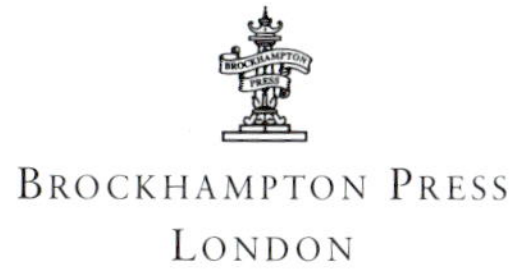

BROCKHAMPTON PRESS

LONDON

THE ORIGINAL Pre-Raphaelite Brotherhood, formed in 1848, is best represented in the work of John Everett Millais, William Holman Hunt and Dante Gabriel Rossetti. These three most prominent members of the brotherhood were disenchanted by the rigid, repetitive teaching methods of the Royal Academy Schools. Looking to the naive style of early Italian artists like Fra Angelico and Giotto for guidance, they rejected what they saw as the extravagant falsehood in the later art of Raphael and his followers and decided to initiate a purer form of representation, transferring nature onto the canvas with highly detailed simplicity. They adopted the

Chinese tradition of painting onto a wet, white canvas with a colour palette much brighter than the dark, heavily varnished canvasses common in the period.

Their innovation and fidelity to nature impressed some, including John Ruskin, the most important art critic of the nineteenth century. But it shocked others, who felt that such a focus on detail led to unseemly or unflattering paintings.

However, detractors were balanced by admirers. The simple and moral tone of the paintings appealed to wealthy industrial patrons who wanted to support a British school of art. It also inspired a whole new generation of artists who adopted the Pre-Raphaelite approach to the sanctity of nature. Arthur Hughes was a notable follower, depicting scenes of youth and lost love in minutely-rendered natural settings. Ford Madox Brown was another disciple. Older in years than Millais, Hunt and Rossetti, he worked closely with all three.

Some of the greatest late nineteenth-century artists used the inspiration of the Pre-Raphaelites to develop new and widely admired styles of painting. John Waterhouse combined a fascination for natural detail with a love of the mythical and the poetic, while Edward Burne Jones developed a semi-mystical style based on medieval fantasy. Scottish artist Noel Paton was known for paintings which recaptured past notions of chivalry and honour. He and Frederick Sandys shared a talent for evocative, smoothly modelled portraits of figures taken from literature and classical history.

These and other painters took up elements of the Pre-Raphaelite legacy to ensure that it survived on into the next century. While the original members separated to pursue a variety of different styles and projects, the ethos of painterly craft and skill that they had established remained as inspiration and guidance to the artists who followed them.

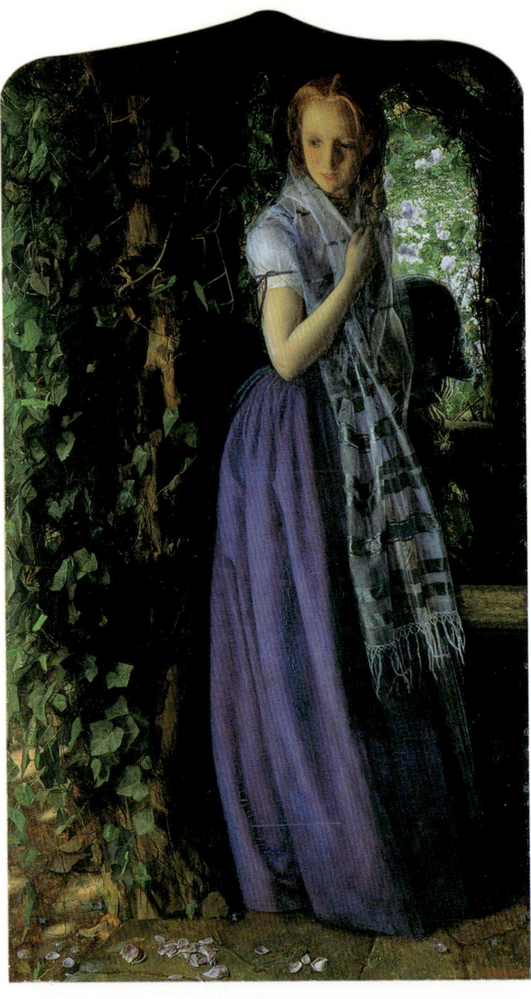

ARTHUR HUGHES (1832-1915)

APRIL LOVE 1855-6

left This picture was much admired when it was first exhibited at the Royal Academy. The combination of richness of colour and attention to detail earned the approval of art critic John Ruskin.

JOHN EVERETT MILLAIS (1829-1896)

OPHELIA 1851-2

overleaf Shakespeare's *Ophelia* was a popular subject for nineteenth century artists, (see Waterhouse) but Millais's version is prominent for its painstaking realism. He copied the acid brightness of the spring landscape exactly from nature, a practice rare in the period.

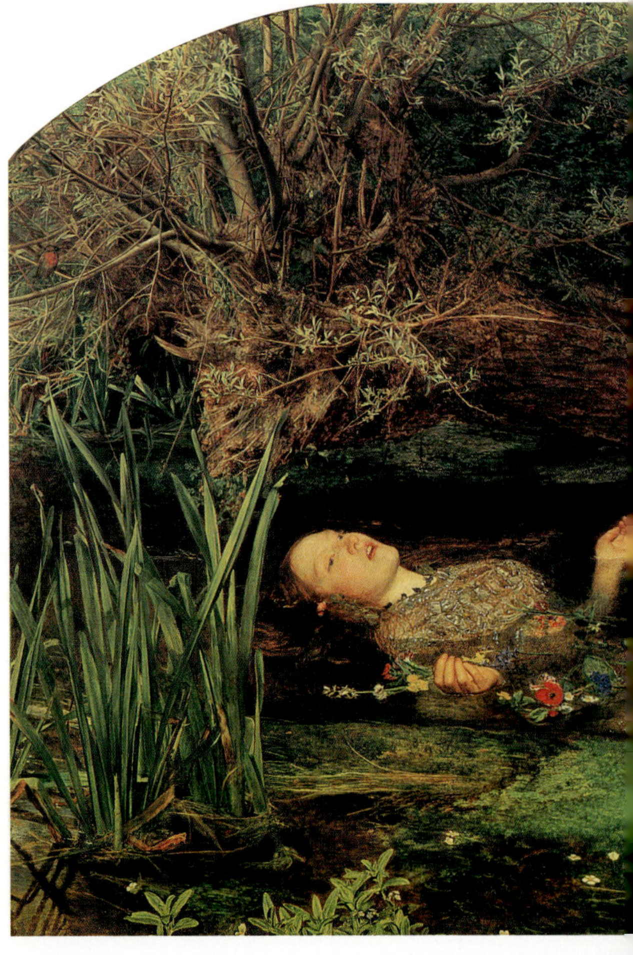

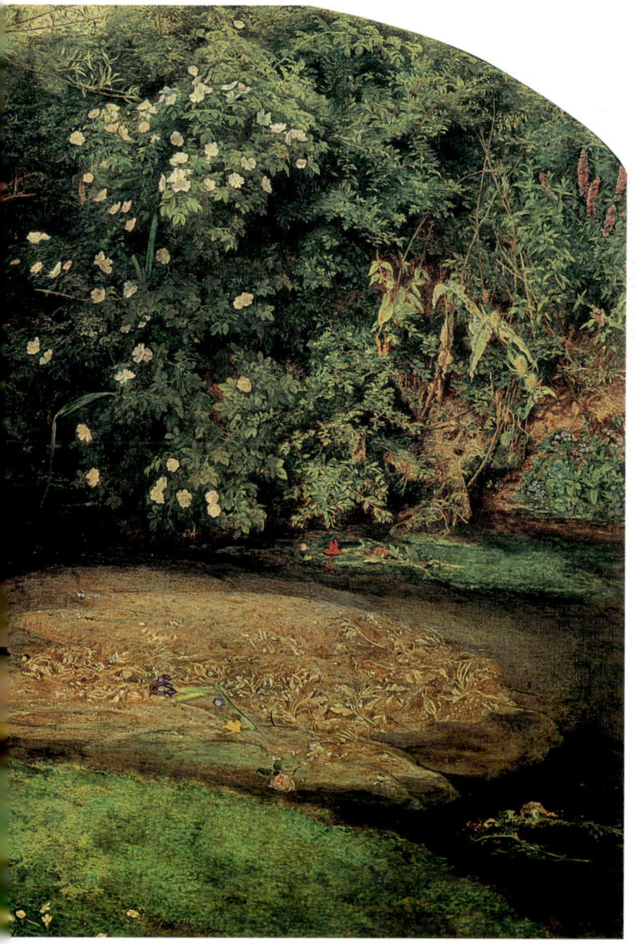

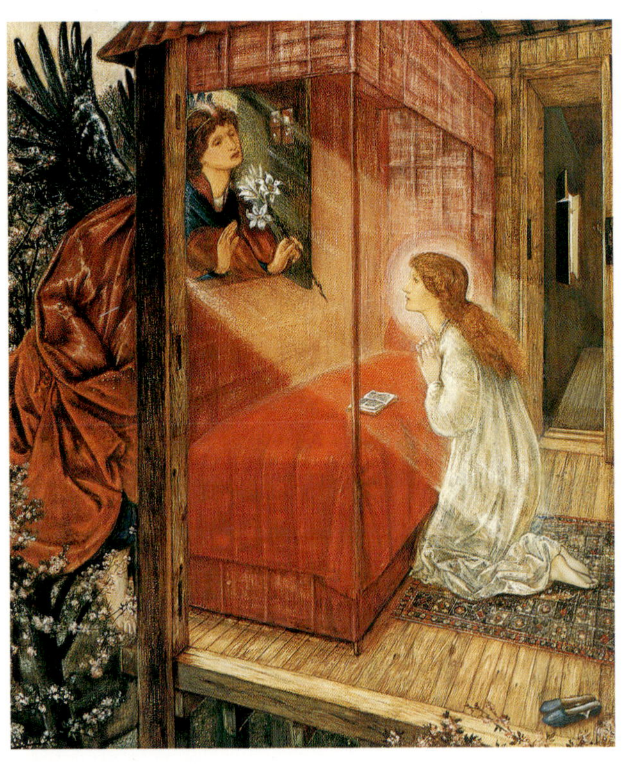

EDWARD BURNE-JONES (1833-1898)

THE ANNUNCIATION C.1863

left Originally entitled *Harmony in Red*, this painting recalls the bold colour schemes of medieval tapestry, while anticipating American artist Whistler's fascination with the uses of colour relationships in painting.

EDWARD BURNE-JONES (1833-1898)

GREEN SUMMER 1868

overleaf Burne-Jones creates a pastoral idyll to suggest the lushness and fertility of high summer. The picture lacks a straightforward narrative, showing the move in painting towards 'art for art's sake'.

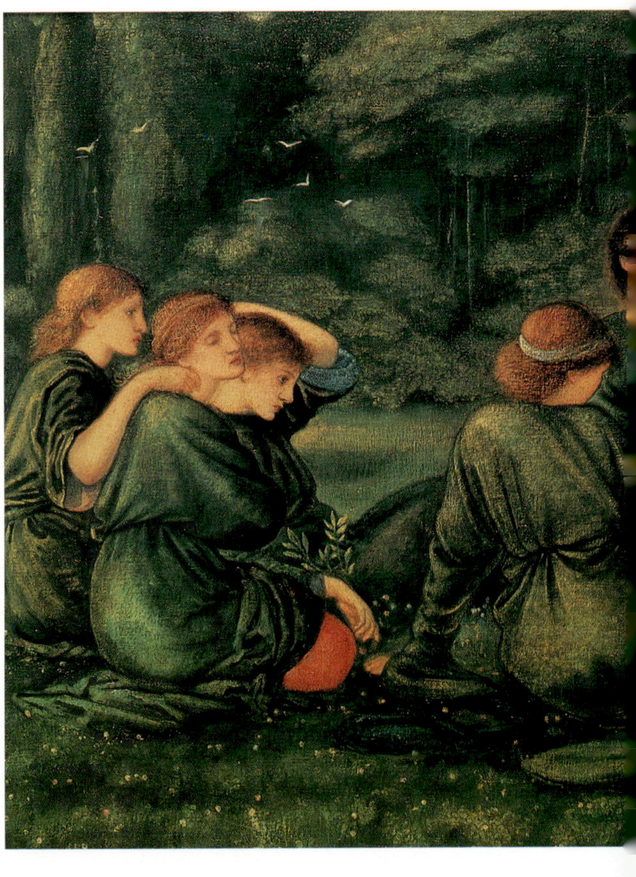

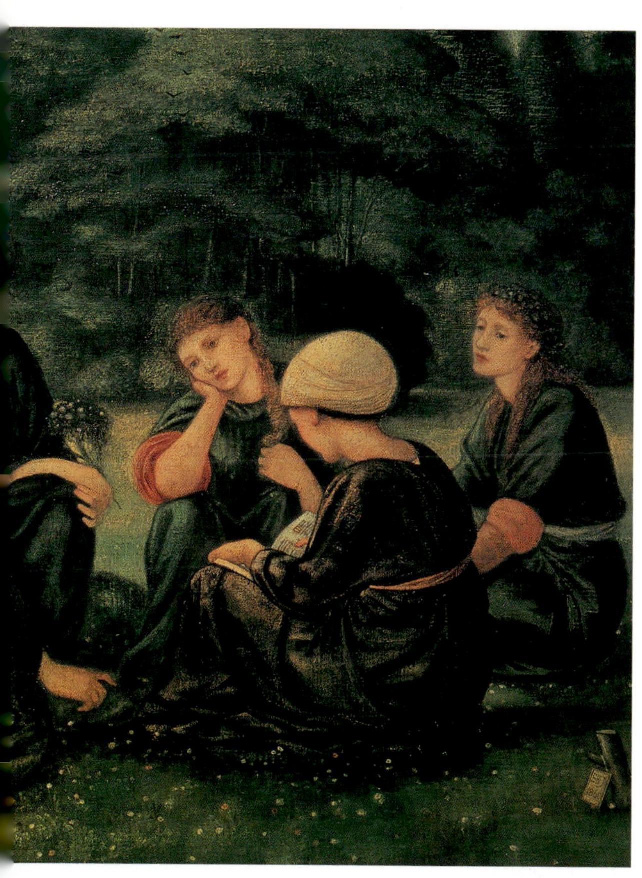

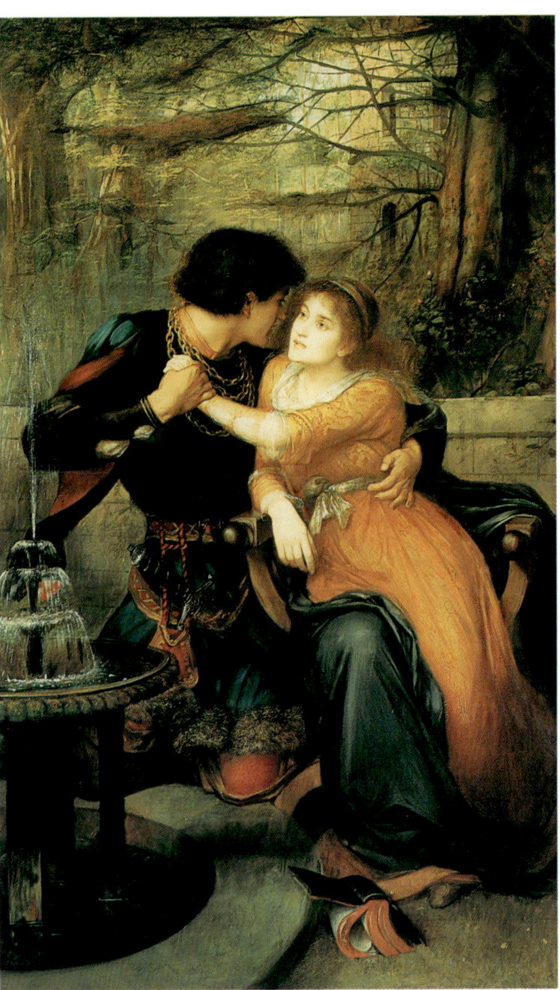

PAOLO AND FRANCESCA 1888

left Hallé uses Dante's myth of the doomed lovers as his theme, focusing the viewer's attention on Francesca's rapt expression. Caught in an adulterous liaison, the couple were consigned to the second circle of hell. The artist creates a tension that invites anticipation of the couple's tragic fall from grace.

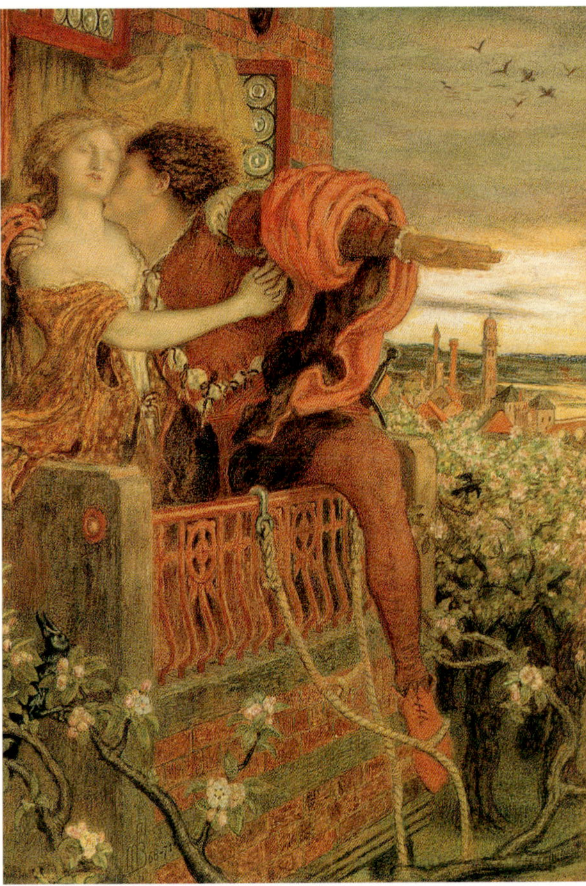

FORD MADOX BROWN (1821-1893)

ROMEO AND JULIET 1868-71

left Madox Brown worked closely with the original Pre-Raphaelite Brotherhood, although never as an official member. He often painted images from literature, particularly Chaucer and Shakespeare. The romantic style of this balcony scene shows the increasing influence of Rossetti on Madox Brown's work.

DANTE GABRIEL ROSSETTI (1828-1882)

THE RETURN OF TIBULLUS TO DELIA 1868

overleaf Delia is shown as a patient and loyal wife, an image of womanhood popular in Victorian painting, that of the patient and loyal wife. The painting originally belonged to Charles Fairfax Murray, an important collector, dealer and benefactor of the period.

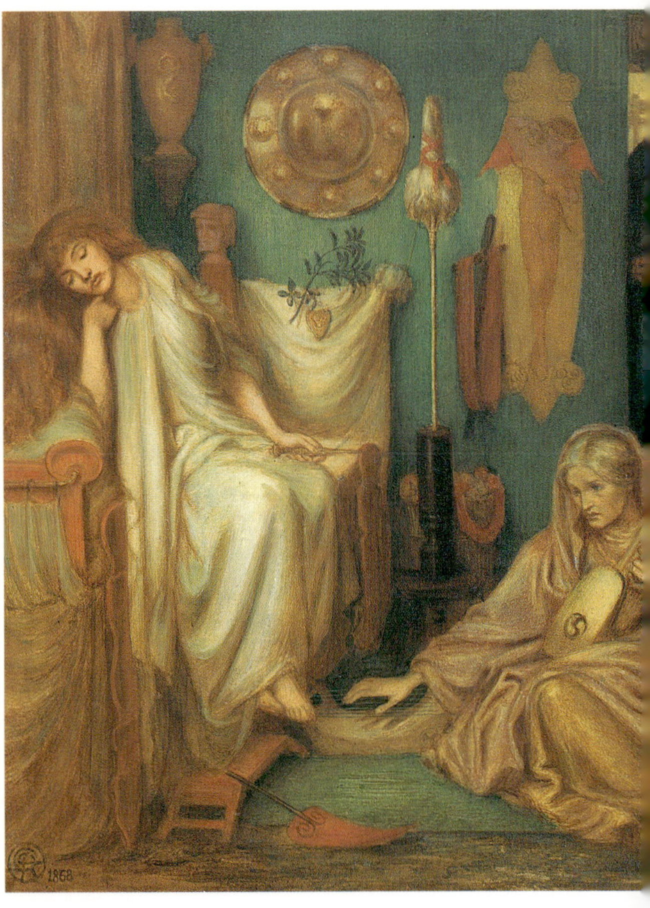

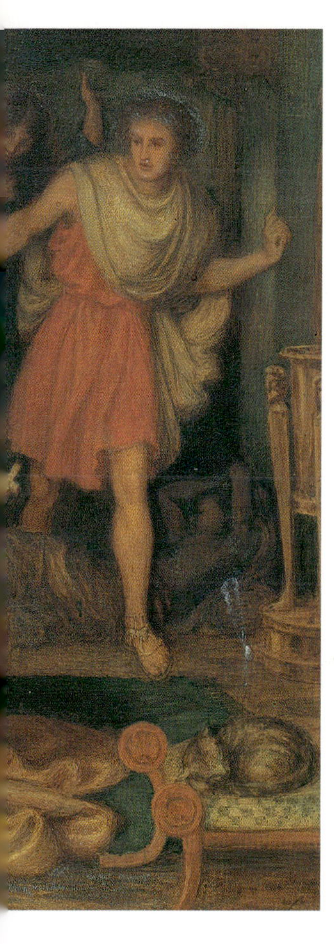

ANTHONY SANDYS (1829-1904)

ORIANA 1861

right Oriana was the heroine of a Tennyson poem, and
Sandys has painted her in a classical landscape. Her
androgynous profile recalls that of ancient Greek sculpture,
while her robes indicate a Venetian influence.

JOHN WILLIAM WATERHOUSE (1849-1917)

A SONG OF SPRINGTIME 1913

overleaf The clarity and richness of Pre-Raphaelite detail
strongly influenced Waterhouse's work. He combined these
with a lyrical, poetic style that made him one of the most
commercially successful artists of the late nineteenth and
early twentieth centuries.

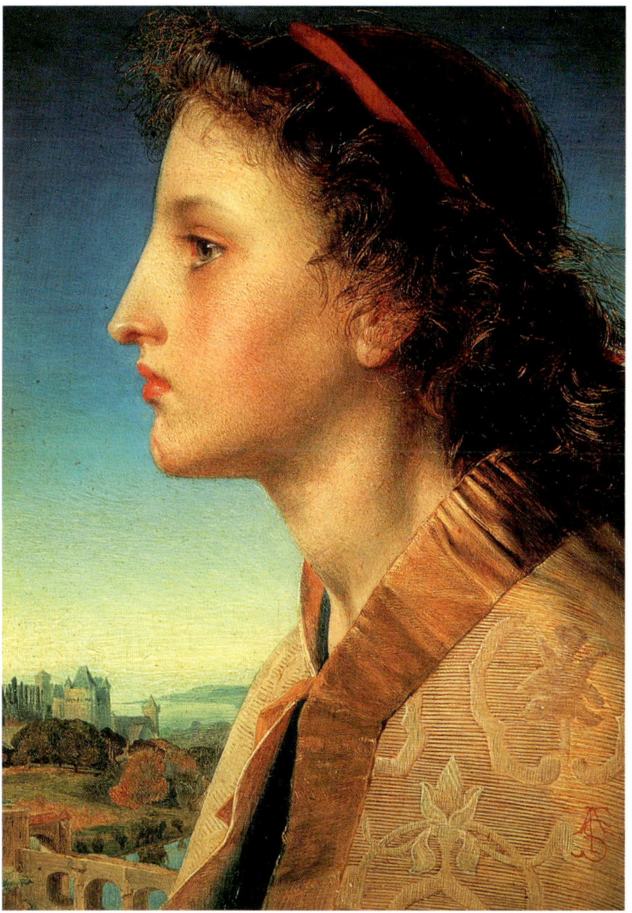

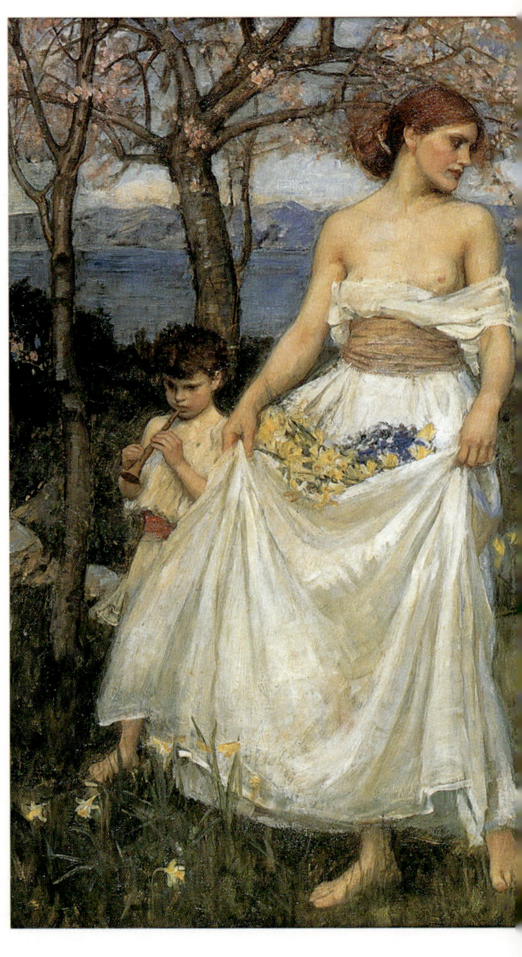

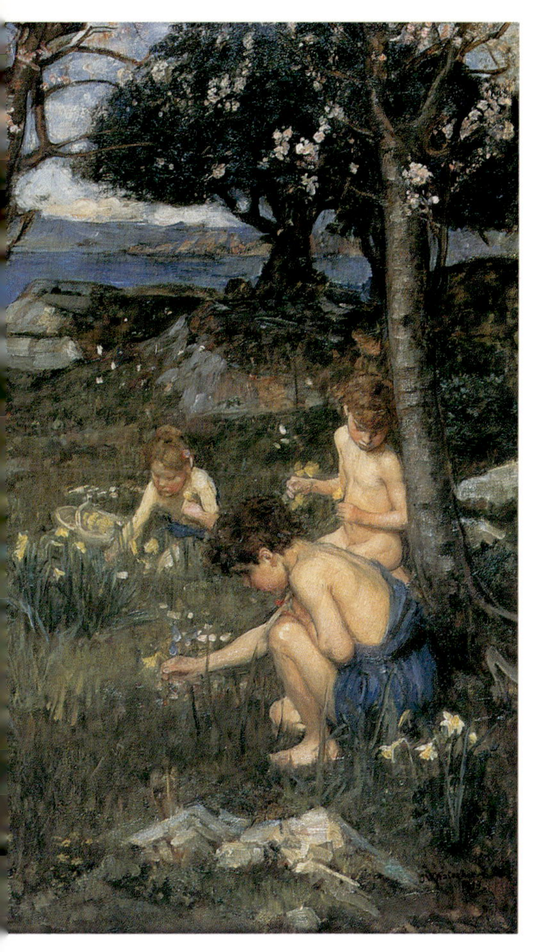

JOHN WILLIAM WATERHOUSE (1848-1917)

OPHELIA 1894

right Waterhouse's version of Ophelia, painted almost half a
century after that of Millais, has a languor and beauty that
divest the subject of tragedy. It was acknowledged as a fine
painting, but critics also felt it lacked the necessary quality
of 'madness'.

JOHN WILLIAM WATERHOUSE (1849-1917)

THE ANNUNCIATION 1914

overleaf The lily was a symbol of purity and holiness popular
with the original Pre-Raphaelite brotherhood, particularly
Rossetti. Waterhouse still uses this element of their pictorial
code well into the next century.

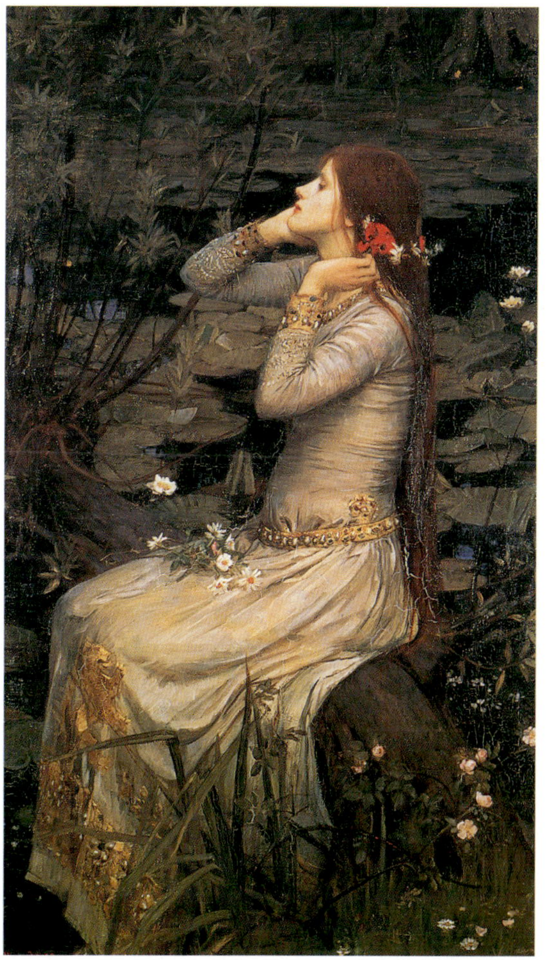

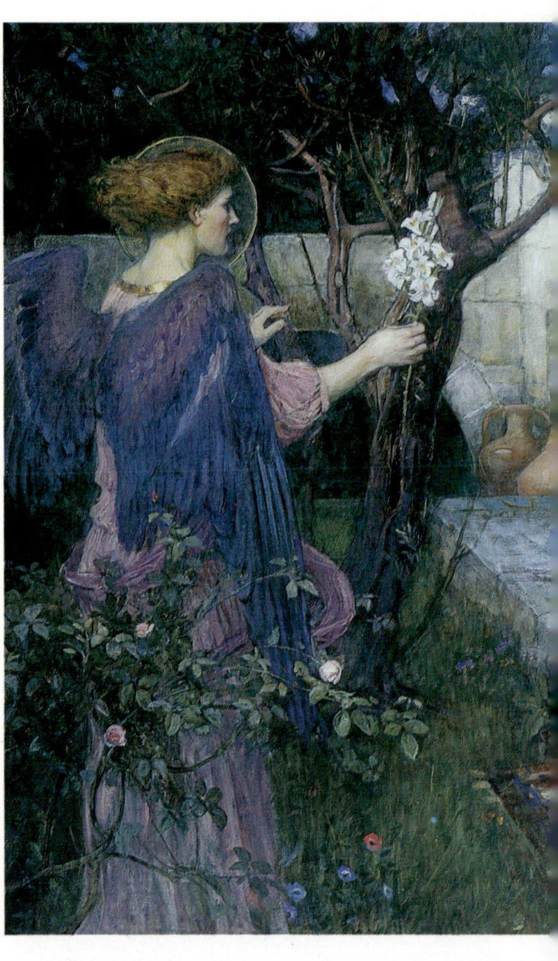

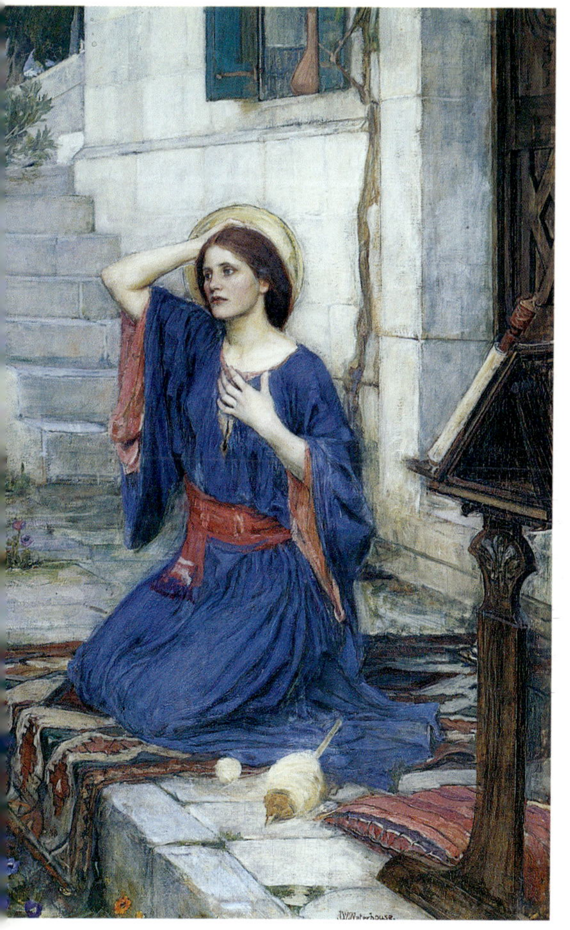

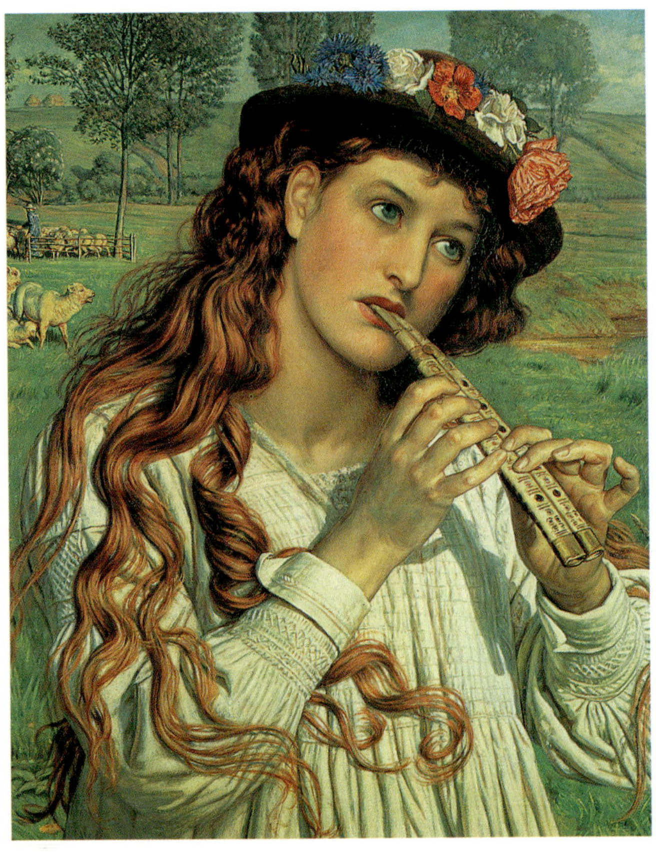

WILLIAM HOLMAN HUNT (1827-1910)

AMARYLLIS, OR THE SHEPHERDESS 1884

left Unlike Hunt's earlier paintings, Amaryllis has no definite
narrative. The artist intended it simply to be a portrait of
feminine youth in a pastoral setting. This content is simpler
than his youthful work, which was thickly punctuated with
symbols and coded moral messages.

JOHN WILLIAM WATERHOUSE (1849-1917)

THISBE OR THE LISTENER 1909

right The tale of Pyramus and Thisbe was popularised by Shakespeare's *A Midsummer Night's Dream*. Waterhouse provides another example of the popularity of the author with the Victorian artist. The artist gives the tale an Assyrian flavour with the eastern-style tiling, and the Nile water-lily motif on Thisbe's robes.

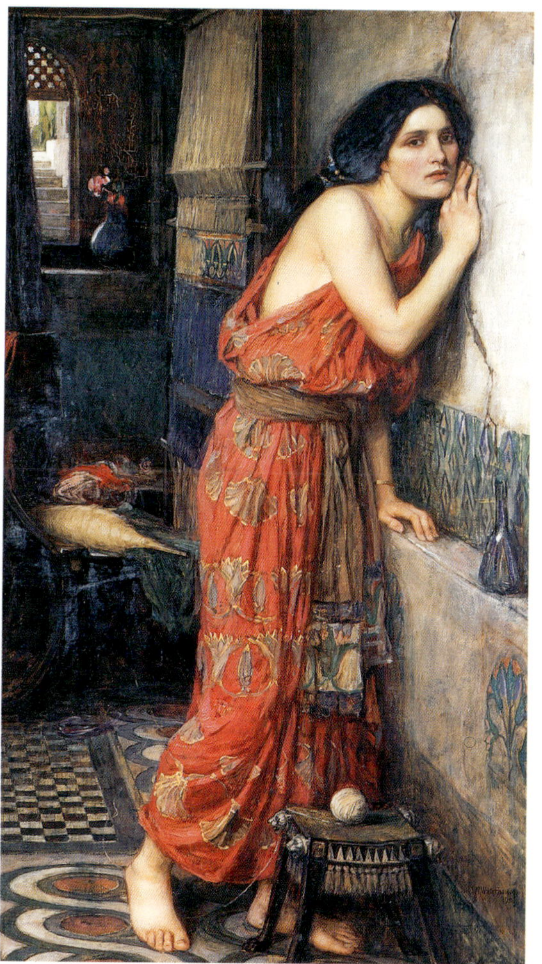

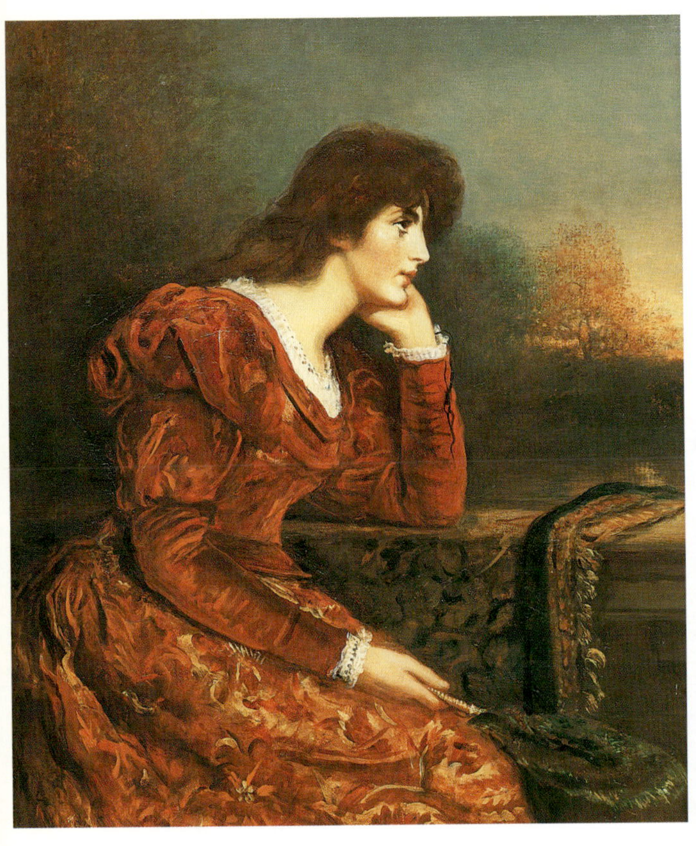

JOHN EVERETT MILLAIS (1829-1896)

I AM NEVER MERRY WHEN I HEAR SWEET MUSIK 1888

left Later in his career, Millais became a very wealthy society portrait artist. This work, although superficially a reference to Shakespeare's *The Merchant of Venice*, is typical of his skill in the genre.

JOSEPH NOEL PATON (1821-1901)

A DREAM OF LATMOS 1879

right The unusual circular frame echoes the orb of the moon

behind the Goddess's head. A smooth paint surface and

subdued colouring reinforce a sense of stillness in the work.

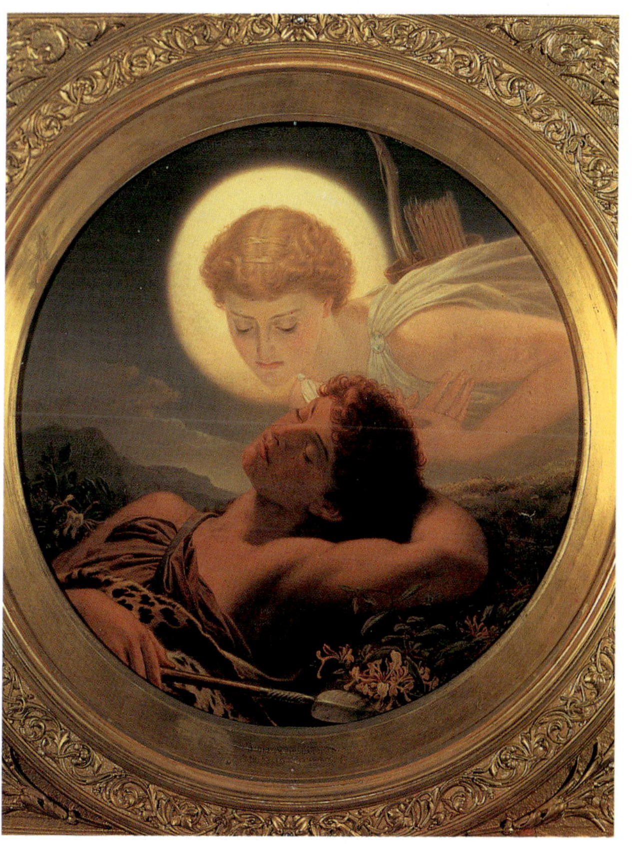

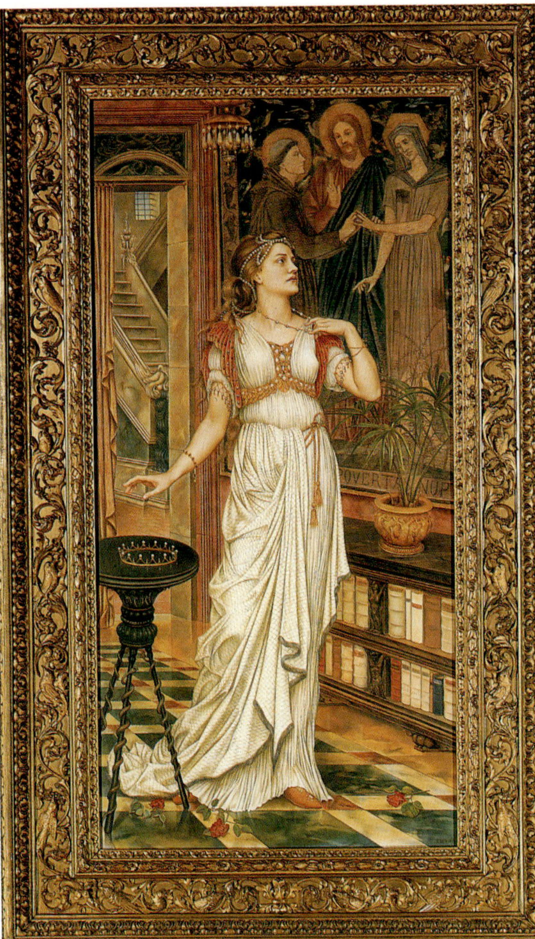

EVELYN DE MORGAN (1855-1919)

THE CROWN OF GLORY 1896

left Evelyn de Morgan and Rossetti's wife Lizzie Siddal
were among the few women artists to adopt a Pre-Raphaelite
style. This richly detailed painting has remained in the hands of
private collectors since its execution.

JOHN WILLIAM WATERHOUSE (1849-1917)

SAINT CECILIA

overleaf This is one of Waterhouse's best-known works,
combining a chaste saintliness of subject with a luxuriant use of
colour and detail.

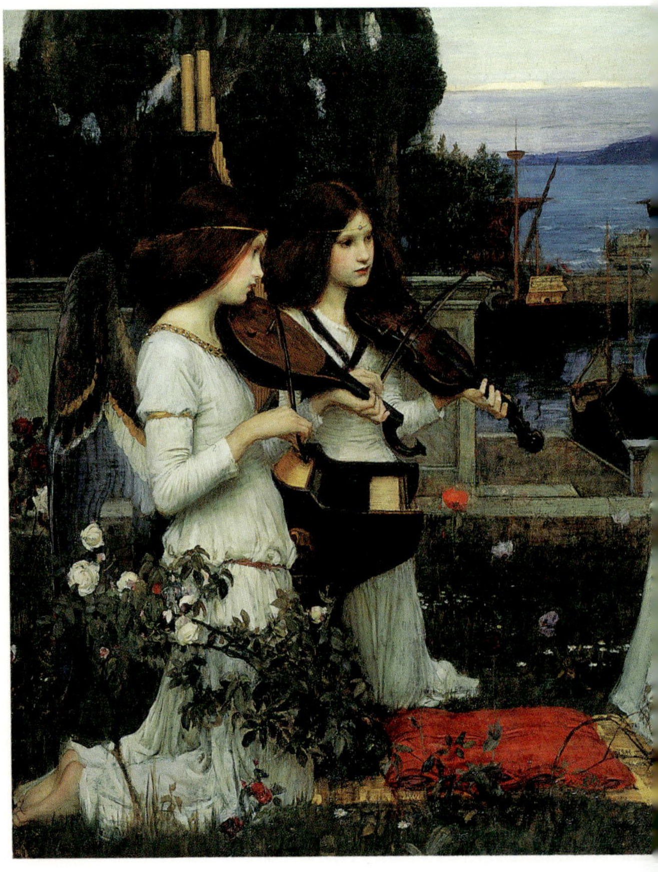

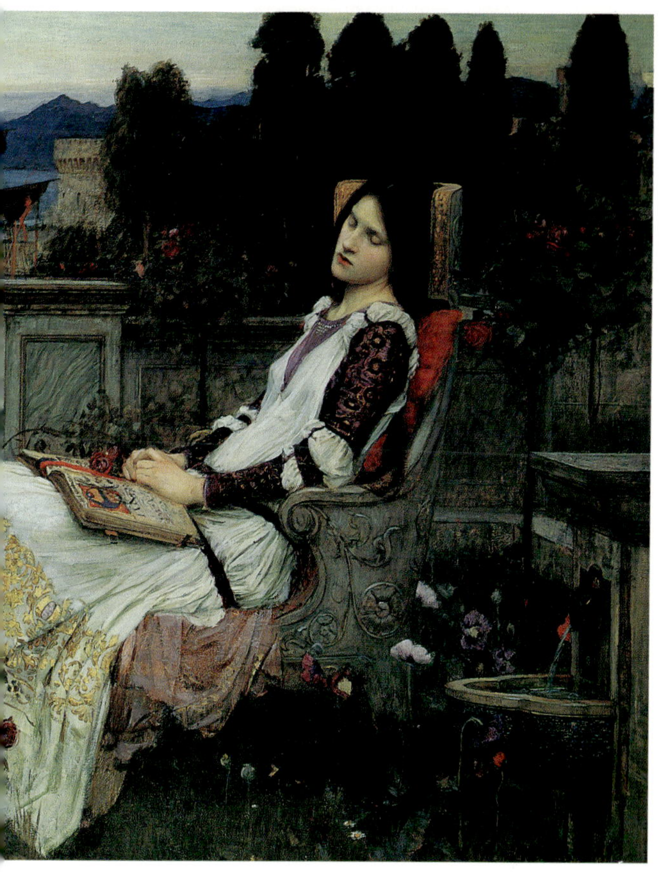

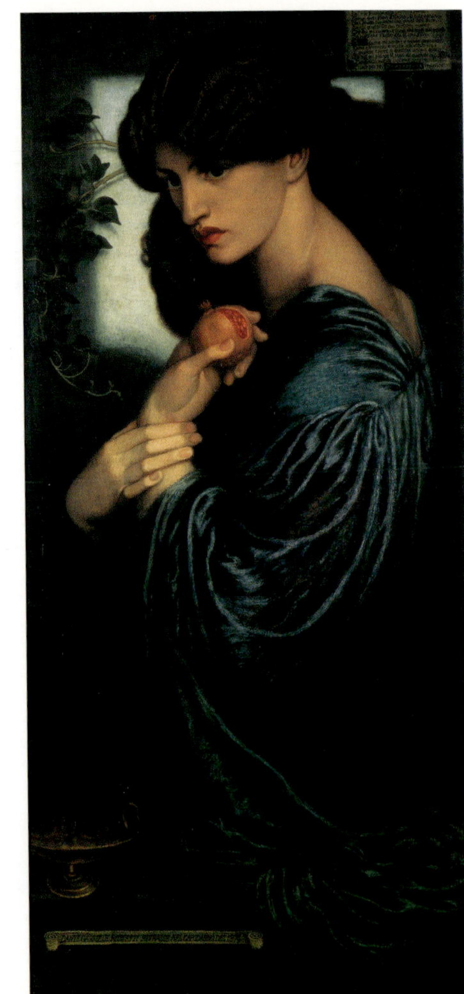

DANTE GABRIEL ROSSETTI (1828-1882)

PROSERPINE 1877

left The model for this picture, and a host of others in this
period, was Jane, wife of William Morris. Rossetti was
deeply in love with her, and the brooding darkness suggest
despair and passion.

JOHN WILLIAM WATERHOUSE (1849-1917)

THE AWAKENING OF ADONIS 1899

overleaf The return of Adonis from the Underworld
symbolised the Spring. Waterhouse blends legend, nature
and ideal humanity in a poetic fantasy.

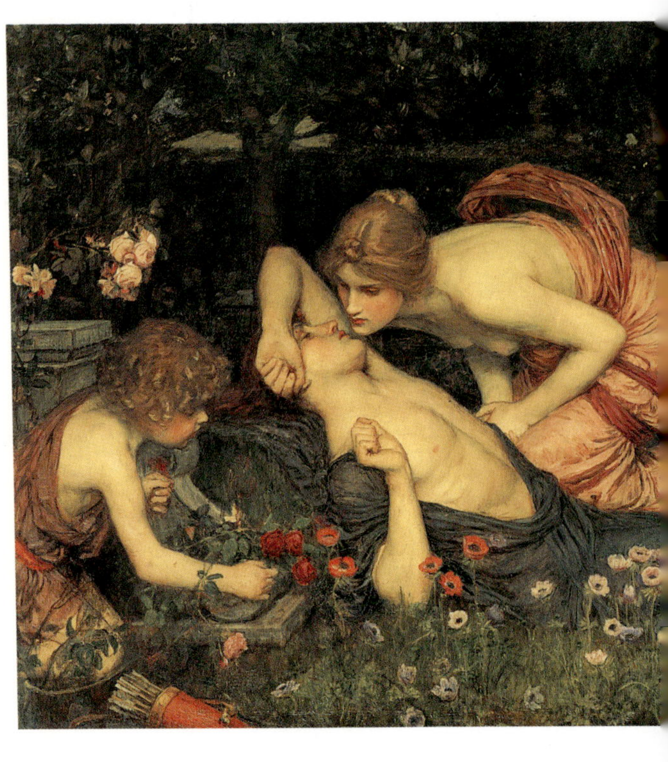

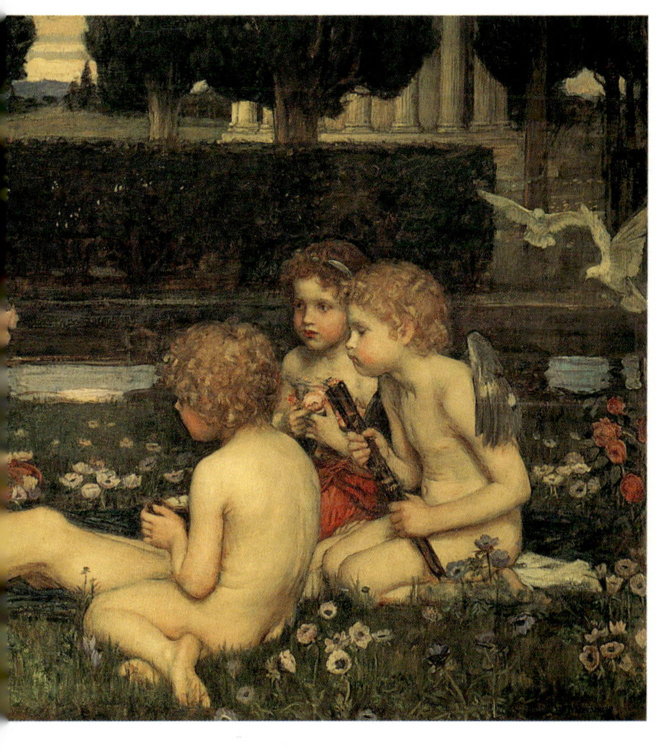

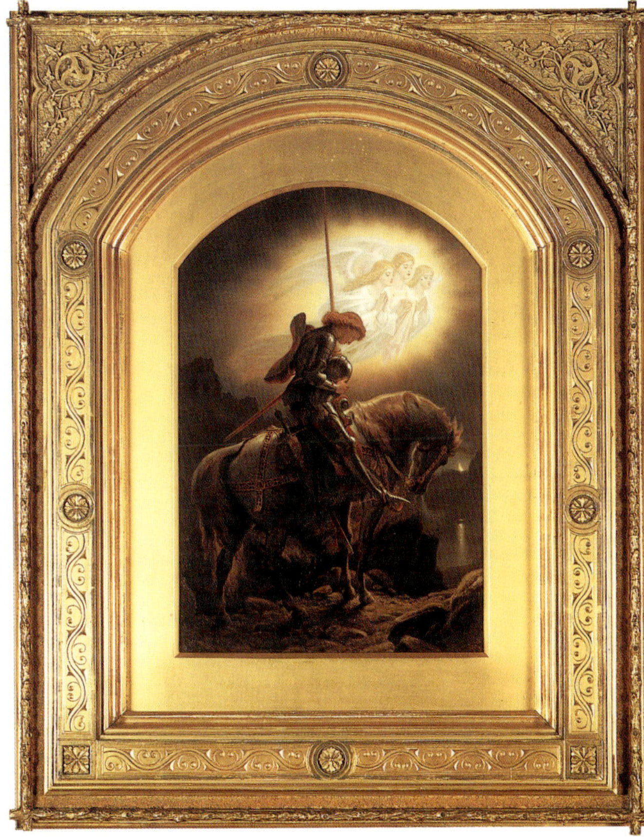

NOEL PATON (1821-1901)

SIR GALAHAD 1879

left Paton shows his Pre-Raphaelite affiliations with a
subject taken from the Arthurian legends that had so inspired
them. Sir Galahad represented the courtliness and integrity to
which they aspired in their art.

JOHN WILLIAM WATERHOUSE (1849-1917)

THE SIREN c.1900

right In Victorian painting, the female figure was often either chaste or aggressively sensual. The beauty of Waterhouse's siren has drawn the exhausted male figure to the perilous sea by the rocks.

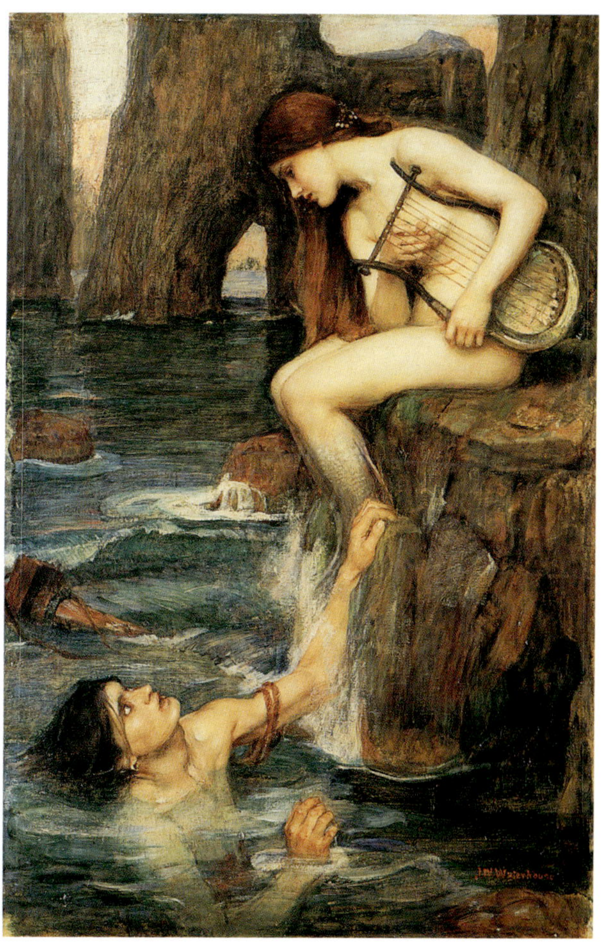
J.W. Waterhouse

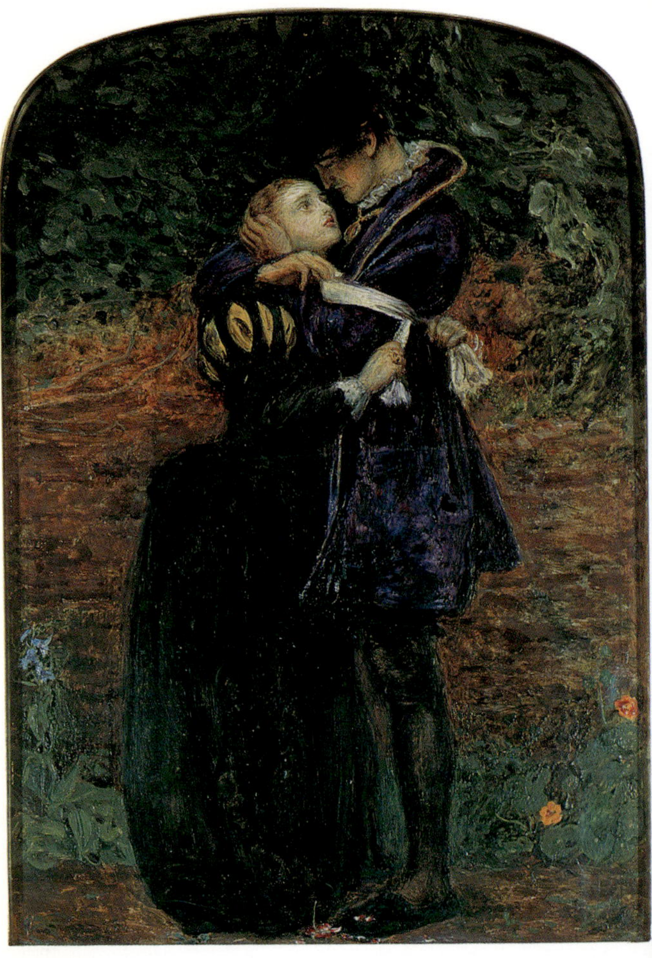

JOHN EVERETT MILLAIS (1829-1896)

THE HUGUENOT 1852

left This is one of Millais's early Pre-Raphaelite works. The theme is both historical and sentimental, a popular combination at the time. The image is of a Huguenot refusing his lover's attempts to make him disguise his faith.

DANTE GABRIEL ROSSETTI (1828-1882)

THE DAMSEL OF THE SANCT GRAIL 1874

right This picture combines the artists skill in painting strong,

handsome female figures with his fascination for Arthurian

legend. The holy grail represents the quest for spiritual

(and in this case artistic) perfection.

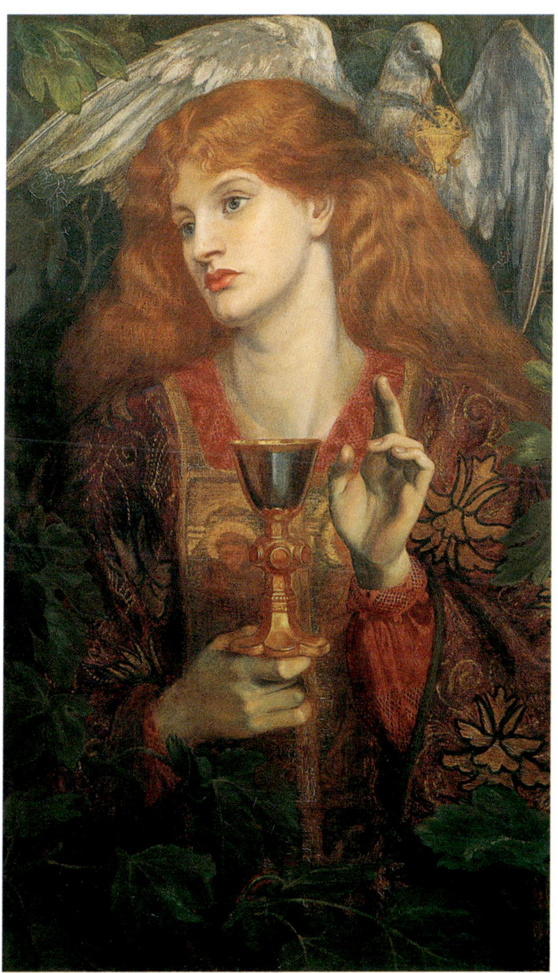

BIBLIOGRAPHY

Quentin Bell   *A New and Noble School*, London, 1982
Gordon H Fleming   *Rossetti and the Pre-Raphaelite Brotherhood*, London, 1967
Tim Hilton   *The Pre-Raphaelites*, London, 1983
Alistair Grieve   *The Art of Dante Gabriel Rossetti*, London, 1981
George Landow   *William Holman Hunt and Typographical Symbolism*, Conn., 1979
Christopher Wood   *The Pre-Raphaelites*, London, 1981

(and assorted monograph catalogues/exhibition publications)

FURTHER READING

William Gaunt   *The Aesthetic Adventure*, London, 1975
Frances Haskell   *Rediscoveries in Art*, London, 1976
Nikolaus Pevsner   *Pioneers of Modern Design*, London, 1962
Graham Reynolds   *Victorian Painters*, London, 1966
Allen Staley   *The Pre-Raphaelite Landscape*, Oxford, 1973
Raleigh Trevelyan   *A Pre-Raphaelite Circle*, London, 1978

OTHER TITLES IN THIS SERIES

Paul Gauguin

Allen Jones

Celtic Art

Salvador Dali

Hokusai

Caspar David Friedrich

Illuminated Manuscripts

First published in Great Britain in 1997 by **Brockhampton Press**
20 Bloomsbury Street, London WC1B 3QA
a member of the **Hodder Headline Group**

ISBN 1 86019 488 5
A copy of the CIP data is available from the
British Library upon request.

Designed and produced for **Brockhampton Press**
by Keith Pointing Design Consultancy.
Text written by Annabel King M.A.

Pictures acknowledgments

The Sleeping Princess, Oriana, A Song of Springtime, The Annunciation
(Waterhouse), Amarylis, Thisbe, I am never Merry.., A Dream of Latmos, The
Crown of Glory, St, Cecilia, The Siren, The Hugenot, The Damsel..,
The Return of Tibullus to Delia, courtesy **Sotheby's Picture Library.**
April Love, Ophelia (Millais), Proserpine,
courtesy of **Tate Gallery Publications Limited.**
The Annunciation (Coley), Green Summer, Paolo and Francesca, Romeo and
Juliet, Ophelia (Waterhouse), The Awakening of Adonis, Sir Galahad,
courtesy of **Christies Images.**

Printed and Bound in Italy by L.E.G.O. Spa.